Succeed Anyway

CREATING THE LIFE YOU WANT TO LIVE

Philip Prinsloo

Succeed Anyway

Published by Philip Prinsloo
Durbanville, South Africa
philipmarkprinsloo@gmail.com

ISBN 978-0-620-89560-6
eISBN 978-0-620-89561-3

2 4 6 8 10 9 7 5 3 1

Layout and cover design by Boutique Books
Printed in South Africa by Bidvest Data

DEDICATION

I dedicate this book to my parents Sean and Mary Williams,
to my wife, Samantha Prinsloo,
as well as to my two daughters Zeike and Zeta Prinsloo.

CONTENTS

ACKNOWLEDGEMENTS

I am cognizant of the fact that we are all the sum total of our past learnings and the contributions of many who have passed along our path or who are still in our lives today. This work is a result of my own continuous learning and personal development, with a further collective contribution from teachers and mentors, advisors, and family and friends. Our meaningful achievements can never be in isolation or without the help and support of others and here I mention just a few people who made this project possible.

I am blessed to still have both my parents alive. Well, my biological father died in a motorcar accident when I was one year old. My mother got married to my stepfather who then became the father who raised me. We are three children, myself and my two sisters. I am the oldest of the three and the age gap between myself and my middle sister is seventeen years. My parents always tried their best to create an enabling environment for me and my sisters to choose whatever we wanted as a career path. They provided guidance but never imposed any career path on their children.

In my younger years, I tried out many ventures that ended up in failure. My parents, however, were always there to support me. They have never highlighted the negatives of the failure but rather the lessons learned. So, as I learned some hard lessons taught to me by the University of Life, they always believed in me and were ready to support my next venture. Today, I still draw from the knowledge and experiences they tried to impart to me. Thank you for not giving up on me when I tried to find my feet in the earlier years of my life.

To my wife, who is always there to motivate me and support me and our two daughters, thank you. She always gives us reality checks and gets us to dissect things and see them from different angles. Thank you for encouraging me to write and publish this book. God really blessed me with you.

To Advocate Shawn Willemse, for your encouragement and advice, and for checking up on me from time-to-time. It is always appreciated.

I want to thank those who worked on this project to make it a reality. Your assistance and advice is appreciated.

Finally, I acknowledge and thank my Heavenly Father for the gift of life and for His faithfulness towards me and my family.

INTRODUCTION

> *Among the greatest tragedies is a person who believes that they aren't meant to win; by winning I mean find their purpose, passion and joy in life. They believe that other people have better DNA or happiness genes or something, but that they themselves are missing a critical chromosome. This is a lie and it is begging to be unbelieved. For, the moment we know the truth about ourselves, we can take both responsibility for our own lives and inspired action to create exactly the life which is our birthright. In other words, you were meant to win.*
>
> **Jacob Nordby**

What if one morning you wake up and are presented with a *"one day only opportunity"* where you can do whatever you want – with no limitations or a lack of resources? You can go anywhere you want, own anything you want, be anything you want for that one day. This will last from the moment you wake up in the morning until midnight of that evening, when things will return to your present state, with you having only a memory of the previous day. Your schedule will probably change immediately, with priorities shifting from your normal daily routine to accommodate your one day adventure presented to you. Every second will count for you. You will probably run through a couple of things you want to achieve for that day. Depending on the person and their interests, some might choose purpose-driven activities, business, relationship and career fulfilment, and others might go for pleasure, entertainment and financial freedom.

As it is an open invitation with no resource limitations, you will get people who will choose an expensive vehicle or vehicles to drive for the day. Others might choose access to top restaurants and eat through the day. Your dream might be meeting top business executives, owning your own company or being the CEO of your dream company for the day; or going on a dream holiday and having access to unlimited treats and entertainment. Perhaps your opportunity would be meeting your role model, acting opposite a famous actor or actress in a movie... and so on. You can fill in the blanks.

Fast-forward to the end of this day and it is back to the state you were in before the opportunity was presented to you. Hopefully, whatever you have thought about achieving for that day contributes to life's purpose and fulfilment – something that will provide meaning in your life. Whatever you'd choose, if such an opportunity were presented to you, if you are not living it today let me ask you what is holding you back from working towards that dream or that life you want to live? What is holding you back from creating that life?

We must debunk the myth that success is only for a certain group of people, while the rest must accept their fate. Therefore, do not measure or compare yourself or your life to someone else in order to determine what success should be for you. Whether you succeed or not is in your hands. Instead of looking at success as a destination that you might hopefully someday achieve, if you are lucky, see it rather as a journey we take daily towards our goals. This journey is based on carefully planned actions that are motivated by what we deem important for us to achieve and believe will create fulfilment for us if we work towards achieving the desired goals. So, the question we should ask then is, "*What is the meaning of success to you?*" What is your personal understanding of success?

The pursuit of success might have a different meaning from person to person. A student may want to get through university successfully; a married couple may want to acquire their first home while also working on having a lasting or successful marriage. For some, it might be gaining financial security, while for another it might be starting or expanding on a business venture and wanting to be successful in that space. For a father, success might be to succeed at fatherhood and to become a better father. For another person, it might be working towards getting a promotion in the company, while someone else may want to increase their fitness levels or lose weight. For many, success means achievement, winning, happiness and progress towards goals – and eventually reaching those goals. Everyone wants to be successful and wants to live a life that is purposeful and fulfilling.

This book is written to help and guide you in order to translate your dreams into a reality. It provides simple steps for you to follow and, if you cooperate with the process, you will be amazed by what you can do and achieve. It is written in an easy-to-understand and practical way, to guide you through the process by using simple examples. The goal of this project is to let you know that you can succeed, to pull out of you that hidden dream and then provide a map or guide for you to get from where you are to where you want to be. For the person who is already living a life driven by purpose, it is a reinforcement, but also a motivation to never stop growing while you are alive.

I want to share with you a definition of success that is very straightforward and easy to understand, but I want to suggest that you read this book to the end and then, when you have completed the book, come back to the definition and read the definition again. If you followed through on each of the steps in this book, which are also very straightforward, you should be able to relate to the definition in a more purposeful way, because you would have followed a process and you should be able to measure your progress and determine whether you are succeeding or not. When you read this definition then, it should have more meaning and purpose for you and be coupled with a clear direction that you can relate to and derive benefit from, making this definition real to you. It will be different to when you read it the first time, which might be now.

Before I share the definition with you, let me reiterate what I said in the first sentence of the previous paragraph: I suggest that you read this book to the end and, when you have completed the book, come back to the definition and read the definition again. This will definitely be worth your while. Let me share the definition below:

My definition of success is as follows:
Achieving a goal you have purposefully planned for. By achieving this goal, you enhance your life's purpose and contribute to a better life for you and those around you.

I strongly believe that whatever we do daily should contribute to our greater purpose and fulfilment in life. Going through the steps suggested in this book will provide guidance to you so that, when you read this definition after you have completed reading this book, it will be from a new frame of reference that is linked to a purposeful and positive creation of your intended direction in life. You will then read the definition with the intent that it contributes to goals that are linked to a life of purpose and fulfilment. I believe that, with the proper guidance and action, anyone can succeed in life. The fact that you are reading this book tells me that you are an intelligent person who knows how to gather relevant resources to better your life. Make the best use of the time that you have left to dwell the earth.

It was a rainy winter's morning and my youngest daughter was watching television while also periodically playing a game on her phone. The room was nice and warm because I'd prepared a fire for them. The rain was pouring down outside. I had got up early in the morning, while everyone was still sleeping, so that I could write and also apply my mind to the new business venture I was embarking on. I walked into the room where she was sitting and I'd decided to sit with her for a while when a thought came to my mind. I was writing a part of this book and my mind and thoughts were still in that space. I thought, "I wonder what my daughters did today that will better their tomorrow?"

> *It isn't sufficient just to want – you've got to ask yourself what you are going to do to get the things you want.*
> **Franklin D. Roosevelt**

I started a conversation with my youngest daughter; my older daughter was still in her room. As I said earlier, the rain was pouring down and the wind was blowing, so it was probably a perfect day to stay in bed or have a "lazy day". I asked my daughter, "Do you enjoy the program you are watching?" She replied yes. "And the game?" She said, with even more excitement, yes, and tried to explain to me some achievements and progression she had made through the levels of the game. I could see that she was happy. A random question popped up in my mind that I kept to myself. The question was: *"How will what she was doing at that moment add value to the bigger picture for her life's purpose?"*

I wanted to steer the conversation in a direction where I could get her to see the value of time and that every moment matters, without spoiling the current moment we were having. I want them to have fun and enjoy life while they are growing up, but I also want them to plant success principles in their system while they are still young. I said to her that these people were probably getting paid a lot of money to act in the episodes, and that I could see that they are good actors and that they were putting their best efforts into the production for others to watch. As we had a brief conversation I said to her, "I wonder what will happen if we reverse the roles? We be the actors and get paid and others spend hours in front of the television watching us." She burst out laughing, but I'd captured her attention.

She saw that I was serious and she actually had some follow-up questions. She'd saved some money and I was trying to let her see that saving money might be smart, but letting that money make more money for you is smarter. This exercise actually hit home because she was saving for a horse – she loves horses. We let her take horse riding lessons weekly. I said to her that buying the horse is one thing, but you need to have money to cover the monthly costs such as stabling, food and costs for the veterinarian, so you need to have a steady stream of income to cover these cost.

I said to my younger daughter, "Someone developed the game you are playing and it seems to me that person is making millions while people are playing the game online.

So, how can we reverse the roles and let someone else play the game for hours while we are getting paid?" What I was trying to sell to her was that someone was probably passionate about something and that someone had had the idea that they'd pursued. Now, millions of people are being kept busy with his or her idea while he or she is making money. I wanted her to see and know that success is an idea away, and that you can have fun through the process. I also wanted her to see that the people she was watching on television, or the person who created the game she was playing, have made a success out of what they are doing and have captured her time for hours, for which they were paid. She dedicated her time to participate in their creations; but how could she do the same or reverse the roles.

As we embark on this journey, I want to encourage you to read this book to the end and implement what you will read; success awaits on the other side.

> *The journey of a thousand miles begins with one step.*
> **Lao Tzu**

It Couldn't Be Done
By Edgar Guest

Somebody said that it couldn't be done
But he with a chuckle replied
That "maybe it couldn't," but he would be one
Who wouldn't say so till he'd tried.
So he buckled right in with the trace of a grin
On his face. If he worried, he hid it.
He started to sing as he tackled the thing
That couldn't be done, and he did it!

Somebody scoffed: "Oh, you'll never do that;
At least no one ever has done it;"
But he took off his coat and he took off his hat
And the first thing we knew he'd begun it.
With a lift of his chin and a bit of a grin,
Without any doubting or quiddit,
He started to sing as he tackled the thing
That couldn't be done, and he did it.

There are thousands to tell you it cannot be done,
There are thousands to prophesy failure,
There are thousands to point out to you one by one,
The dangers that wait to assail you.
But just buckle in with a bit of a grin,
Just take off your coat and go to it;
Just start in to sing as you tackle the thing
That "cannot be done," and you'll do it.

GARBAGE IN, GARBAGE OUT!

>

The term *garbage in, garbage out* is a term that many of you, if not all of you, are probably familiar with. In short it is referred to as *GIGO*. I will get back to GIGO in a minute.

My grandfather used to tell me stories when I was a young boy but many times, at the end of these stories, he would bring across a life lesson. As we were driving into town one day, we saw circus animals and he said to me that the circus was in town. He stopped next to the road and asked me to particularly look at the elephant. I had seen elephants on television or in books, but that was the first time I saw an elephant in the flesh. He asked me whether I thought that the elephant is a strong animal or not. I said that such a large animal must surely be a strong animal.

He then brought my attention to the elephant's feet. A piece of chain was strapped on one of the elephant's legs and the chain was fastened to a small pole in the ground that looked not very strong. As the car stood next to the road, he said to me, "Take a good look, and think about this. Get this picture

in your mind. When we get home we will talk about it again."
Well, our afternoon talk for later that day was determined by
the picture we saw that morning and particularly the picture
of the elephant, and I wondered what my grandpa wanted
to talk about. Being a young boy, my mind was leaning more
towards tickets to go and see the circus.

Back to GIGO. I grew up in a rural town with gravel roads
and when I went to secondary school my parents moved to a
small holiday town near the beach. When I attended school
we did not work with computers or have a computer lab at
school, so the first time I heard about the term GIGO was
in my computer science class while attending university. This
acronym suggests that bad or wrong input will result in bad
or wrong output. So, what you put in is what you get out.

That afternoon, grandpa and I sat on the stoep and he
said to me, "The elephant can easily pull that chain with
the pole out of the ground and be free. But, because of how
the elephant was programmed since he was a baby elephant
growing up, he believes that, even though he is now older
and much stronger, he cannot break free. When he was small
he might have struggled to pull the chain with the pole from
the ground, and eventually he gave up. Years later, his mind
is keeping him in the same space where he was when he was
a child, even though he has now grown strong."

I like what Solomon said in the book of Proverbs: As a man thinks in his heart, so he is! The elephant thinks that he cannot break loose when he is strapped by the chain. That was put into his mind since he was small. That is how he was conditioned, so when they chain him to the pole, they know he will not break loose because that is what was put into his mind when he was small, and that is the output they are still getting today.

Grandpa said to me that many people are like this elephant. They are programmed by their parents, society, surroundings, communities, teachers and other influences that they have allowed to shape them since when they were small, and in many instances these influences were negative and were only the views and opinions of other people. He introduced me to a quote from Mahatma Gandhi that says: *"I will not let anyone walk through my mind with their dirty feet"*. My grandpa was a school principal, and he used to explain things to me in an easy and understandable manner, many times through a story.

One of the largest gaps between individuals who are successful and individuals who are not successful is their thinking and belief system. So, your mind can either keep you small or propel you towards greatness. That is why you get people with many educational achievements who are still studying to further their education even more, yet they remain in junior positions. You then get the individual who barely made it through university or, in some instances, without any formal education or degree, yet they manage the highly-educated person or own the business. Change your mind and your belief system and you will change your future.

The correct mindset and correct thinking is a very important ingredient for success. The good news is that winning mindsets, winning mentalities, are developed. Let me put it to you like this: *our mind is the battleground.* Whatever thoughts you allow to influence your mind can influence your life. A successful business was once a thought. Someone took that thought and believed they could make it a reality – and they did. If you think you can, you will. Your thoughts will either make you or break you. Change your thoughts and you will change your life. What you think becomes your reality.

So, the question is, are you focusing more on negative thoughts that influence your beliefs or positive thoughts that influence your beliefs. In other words, what are you feeding your mind? This is an important question because what we feed our mind with will take up more space in our mind and will grow to become our memory. This influence, whether negative or positive will soon be the portrait that is reflected in your day-to-day life.

So, how can I influence my mind to influence my life? We do that through a process we call renewing our mind. You therefore don't have to conform to your current state of your mind and thinking; instead, you can transform that by renewing your mind and thinking patterns. As we feed the body with food, we feed the mind with good, positive, motivational material that will grow and challenge us for the good. The era we find ourselves in further spoils us with options. Free motivational YouTube videos, good books covering a wide range of topics and advice, free seminars, mentorship programs and the like are available to us all. Believe you can be successful and you will be successful. No matter what it is, how small or big, if you truly believe you can achieve something, you will; the how to achieve it will come. It all starts with you believing that you can.

Henry Ford, the inventor of the Ford motor car said, "Whether *you think you can, or you think you can't – you're right"* You create the limitations in your mind.

> *We are addicted to our thoughts. We cannot change anything if we cannot change our thinking.*
> **Santosh Kalwar**

I suggest that you make time daily to read positive motivation material as well as something that might assist you with your career, business or whatever you deem to be an area in which you want to expand your knowledge on. Someone told me once that, if you do not maintain something, it will deteriorate. This is very true. You might be fit and in good shape today, but if you stop exercising and start to feed your body junk food, you might become unfit and gain some weight again and it will reflect through your body. Point is, consistency is the key. If you don't look after yourself and certain areas of your life, they will deteriorate. You don't live off last week's food, you eat daily. The same should apply for every area of your life.

Someone shared with me that our memory is like a bank account. In order to make a withdrawal, you need to make a deposit. Always make time to make deposits into your memory bank account so that, when a need arises to make a withdrawal, you can do so with comfort and not find yourself with a message in return: *insufficient funds,* or, as in this case, *insufficient memory.* Always make time to make *positive* deposits into your memory bank account. Never see it as time wasted. Your success depends on this. This simple act might change your life forever. Make it your business to invest in good books that will expand your knowledge and provide you with the guidance and motivation to achieve. Listen to motivational videos and tapes. Minimize your time around negative people who always make excuses for not being able to achieve.

I want to reiterate what I said earlier, since this is very important. Successful businesses, careers or relationships started with an idea or thought. Every man-made thing exists because someone believed that they could convert their thought or idea into a reality and was willing to pursue it against all odds. The company that you work for was in someone's mind. Someone believed and pursued the dream and the result is a vacancy in that company that is filled by you. So, believe you can – and you will.

My grandpa, through his storytelling, tried to work on my belief system by making deposits into my memory bank. I was still young when he died. As I grew up, I realized that I need to take responsibility for my life. I am the captain of this ship. My mother took us to church every Sunday and she made me listen to the sermon. One day, a preacher introduced the Message Bible to us, and he read a scripture in Ecclesiastes 10:2-3 that said: *Wise thinking leads to right living; Stupid thinking leads to wrong living. Fools on the road have no sense of direction. The way they walk tells the story: There goes the fool again!*

This scripture spoke to me and woke up the giant within me. This might sound simple, but I immediately could relate to what was said in this scripture. I could relate it to decisions I made based on my thinking and what outputs I got from the decisions I made. I could relate it to my response to the outputs I received from these decisions that I made. I could relate it to a story that my grandpa told me about an elephant and the chain around his leg attached to a pole in the ground. This made me hungry to develop myself and to gain more knowledge.

I then realized that my thought patterns and belief system were a result of me feeding my mind with certain content and that the outputs were directly related to what I had fed my mind over the years. So, in order to get a different output I needed to change my input. I needed consistently to feed my mind with principles of success and positive motivation until it impacted on my belief system and influenced my output to be positive as an automatic reaction.

What I'm suggesting is that, if you cannot see yourself accomplishing the goal, if you do not believe that you can succeed, the probability of you failing is great. You will start off with double-mindedness, filled with doubt and excuses as to why it might not work, instead of working towards the goal as if failure is no option and with the confidence and a belief system that propels you to succeed. And, if challenges arise, you'll just give up and say things such as, *"I knew from the start or I had my doubts,"* instead of dealing with the challenges and moving forward to succeed. Remember that none of us are exempt from challenges or trouble, but a successful person will face trouble or challenges head on, deal with them and move on.

> *There is little difference in people, but that little difference makes a big difference. The little difference is attitude.*
> *The big difference is whether it is positive or negative.*
> **W. Clement Stone**

You are a product of your thoughts and you will continue to become what you think, so change how you see yourself if the picture is negative. And, if it means breaking away from negative people and filling your free time with self-development activities – reading motivational material, listening to motivational material, studying your industry or an industry of interest to you, and building lasting relationships – you do so.

From the second that you're in this world by
By Erin Hanson

From the second that you're in this world,
They tell you what is "fair",
The questions you're allowed to ask,
And the ones you wouldn't dare.
Placed on the path they've paved for you,
Life pushes you along,
Without the chance to stop and think,
If it's right where you belong.
But beyond your pathway's edges,
Is where living really starts,
A land of risks and danger,
And a land of broken hearts.
They'll tell you you should fear this land,
That there's no good there at all,
As they live their lives as they've been taught,
Behind expectation's wall.
But the best people you'll ever meet,
Have wandered off their track,
Found themselves along the way,
And have no need wander back.
So forget about life's road map,
Follow your heart at any cost,
For you'll never truly find yourself,
If you're too scared to get lost.

Taking Responsibility

I entered a building one day where I attended a meeting and my eyes caught something very interesting. It was a sticker with a message at the bottom of the mirror. I stared into the mirror while reading the message which was as follows: "Meet the person responsible for your safety". Guess what, that person in the mirror was me. The message was linked to a campaign around safety and security. I want to use this same example and change the writing on that sticker at the bottom of the mirror to: "Meet the person responsible for your success". The person responsible for your success is you.

You might have heard someone say, or you might have read before, that you need to take full responsibility for your life. What does it mean to take full responsibility for your life and how do you take full responsibility for your life? We will answer this questions in this chapter.

If you want to be successful in reaching the goals that you have identified and set for yourself, it will start with a decision to take full responsibility to do so. In order to succeed in life, being a responsible person who will take full responsibility to succeed is an ingredient or a necessary attitude to have. Making the decision to take responsibility for your life and its outcomes will transfer you from a mode of being a victim to becoming victorious.

Let me take a step back because I know that people who read this book will be from different backgrounds and will find themselves at different stages of life. Some are already self-starters and motivated individuals and are climbing the ladder of success and are just continuously looking for self-development and reinforcement for what they are already implementing. Others might be starting out on this new journey. Some are trying to deal with a failure that set them back while others are down and out and don't even think they can bounce back. Guess what? It doesn't matter where you find yourself on your journey. Whether life happened to you, good or bad, your next steps, decisions and actions will determine your future outcome. So, if a better tomorrow depends on your decisions and actions of today, you might as well make the decisions and take the actions that will put you in a better place tomorrow.

I mentioned to you in the previous chapter about my grandpa, who always tried to make time to tell me stories but would end each story off with some life lessons. I also had an uncle who I saw once a year when they came to visit, and when he came to visit he would have long talks with me. He called me by my second name. He would ask me, "Mark, what

did you do today to ensure that you are better off tomorrow?"
I was young and sometimes did not understand what he
meant. I was still in primary school then. He would then go
on to explain, but he'd make sure that I got the message.
I could see that he lived and applied the principles that he
shared with me. He also went to be with the Lord years ago
but, during one of my lasts visits with him before he died, he
said to me, *"Remember this: the Mark who will be 50 or 60 years old
one day is dependent on the Mark who is in his teens now. Make sure
that you are making it easier for him then; so do your best while you
are at the peak of your life."* That stayed with me.

His wife today is still enjoying the fruits of his labour in
her old age. When I visit her, she will always refer back to
him and how he taught life lessons and helped many. She was
over 80 years when I wrote this part of the book, and she was
still looking good, going to the gym and living a fulfilled live.
I quoted what he said to me above because I could see this
being portrayed even after his death. He ensured that the
older him who was dependent on the younger him was taken
care of, not just for him but also in the eventuality of him not
being there to take care of his family anymore. Because he
had planned ahead, they were taken care of. It went beyond
him and today his wife enjoys the fruit of decisions that were
taken many years ago.

In your pursuit of success, it will be required of you to be
honest with yourself. Taking responsibility for your life will

allow you to take control of important aspects in your life, and not leave it up to others to steer you in a direction they think is best for you. If you think about it, if you take responsibility for your life you can create order in the areas you view as chaotic and steer it into a direction you want to take. Making a commitment to yourself to take full responsibility for your life while also examining yourself in an honest and truthful way, and then implementing the chapters that will follow while committing to the process, will enrich your life tremendously and will impact on generations to come. Through the process, you will learn, grow and create the life you want.

> *The moment you take responsibility for everything in your life is the moment you can change anything in your life.*
> **Hal Elrod**

A sad reality today is that many people blame everyone and everything around them – except for themselves – for where they find themselves at this stage of their lives. They blame their job, family, time, resources, friends, their boss and so many other things. Let me suggest to you that the one person responsible for your success is you.

The sooner we take full responsibility for our lives, the sooner we can do what we need to do to succeed. This will require us to make a conscious effort to look at ourselves, to be honest with ourselves and to choose to take full responsibility for our lives and where we are currently. We will need to decide what we want, to plan carefully while employing success principles, and then commit to the process of implementation. This might not be easy – it might even be uncomfortable – but, if you want to be successful, you will have to make choices that might be in your view difficult. In the long run, however, it will impact your life positively. It takes courage to be successful, but the good news is that you can be successful if you choose to succeed.

It doesn't make sense to find yourself in a space where you are not happy with where you have ended up in life but to do nothing to move from where you are to where you would like to be. If you want to remain where you are, you don't have to do anything except to make peace with your choice of not attempting to better your life or reach for your dreams. However, doing nothing might even worsen your situation. No movement will eventually propel you backwards because, as you stand still, the world is moving forward.

To not be satisfied or happy and not do anything about it also does not make sense. You can just as well be courageous, choose to go after your dreams, plan carefully, commit to the dream, work towards your dream one day at a time, and eventually live the life you want because of taking action today by going after your dreams that you have translated into achievable goals. Guess what? It is a choice you have to make and the sooner you choose to succeed the sooner you can live the life you have designed and created for yourself. Oh yes, you have created the life you are currently living and the life you want to live in the future is determined by what you do now, every day.

You will always get the people who will still try to convince you that it is really not their fault that they did not advance to where they wanted to be in life. It was circumstances out of their control or a certain event that happened to them. But, if it were not for this unexpected circumstance or event, then they probably would have succeeded. They have blamed their parents for the past 20 years for not sending them to university and now they can't get the promotion or job they really want. They don't have time and therefore they cannot exercise. They do not have the money to start a business. Their boss doesn't like them and is treating them badly, which is now influencing circumstances at home, which has a ripple effect on other things.

> *Take a method and try it. If it fails, admit it frankly, and try another. But, by all means, try something.*
> **Franklin D. Roosevelt**

Well, things happen that might not always be in your favour or an unforeseen circumstance might hit you, but you have full control over your response to what happens to you. Part of taking full responsibility includes choosing how you will view and respond to any circumstance that might come your way. Part of the road to success and part of growing will require you to deal with disappointments along the way, but how you view disappointments and events that happen to you, and how you respond to them, is the determining factor for you; where you either learn from them or not. If the outcome was not according to your plan, instead of blaming or making excuses, choose rather to accept responsibility, assess the situation and plan carefully what you will do next. Whatever the outcome you are facing, you choose to learn from events, make the changes you need to make and move on. In an instance where the outcome is of a nature that requires of you to start over or change course, carefully assess the situation and then do the necessary. If you have chosen to take full responsibility for your life, giving up is never an option.

There are things you do not have control over, and one of these things is being born into this world to a particular family. You also do not have control over your past, but you have control enough to influence your future. All of us have different difficulties that we have to face or that we are confronted with. These are situations or events that we strongly believe are contributing factors to where we find ourselves currently in life. You might even find yourself facing some of these difficulties as you read this book.

I recently played a game called *Rummikub* with my wife and while we were playing a brief thought passed across my mind. I thought that the game was a lot like life. I have been dealt 14 tokens that I need to use to play to the best of my ability. I need to build certain patterns and pack these patterns out until I have no tokens left, but many times I find myself with more than the 14 tokens that I started out with. In some instances, I progress to the point where I only have 2 or 3 tokens to put out or build with and soon I find myself with 7 or 10 tokens again.

I need to continuously think and plan in order to stay in the game and to play effectively with the tokens I have. I must make do with what I have and manoeuvre myself through the game to the best of my ability. In some instances, I need to pack out or let go, and in other instances I need to pick up. Whatever I do, I need to play to the best of my ability with the tokens I have. Sometimes, I get rewarded with a joker, which can give me an advantage, depending on how I use it.

My point is that you have been dealt life and it does not matter where you started or where you find yourself; it does matter how you play your next hand to the best of your ability to get to where you want to be. If you look at the game I am using as an illustration, if I complain it doesn't help me or change circumstances for me. What brings change is me taking action and playing the game to the best of my ability. It is the same in life. Complaining about your past or where you are will not bring change. Planned action and consistency will bring change.

Let me also say that, if the circumstance or the event you are facing was the main factor or ingredient for success, many people would have failed or not have reached success. Instead, it is how we view and respond to the circumstance or events that will determine whether we are successful or not.

Even failing is an event. It is not final but is rather temporary, and our response to it determines our success in life.

We make the circumstance or the event the determining factor. We choose not to start something or to give up on something because of the circumstances. We choose to not try again. We allow failure to derail us from our end goal. But, if you study successful people they will tell you how many times they have failed and that failure did not stop them from either starting again or just correcting the mistake or failure and moving on. Many others have overcome these circumstances and if they can, you can too. I mean, you do not even have to go far. Some of these people are around you. The person attending church with you who owns his own business and is doing well; your school mate who once played with you when you were in school and who is now working for a top firm after attending university and eventually completing a professional qualification; your brother or sister who has advanced to supervisor at work; your neighbour who started a corner shop and now already owns three of these shops.

> *Failure should be our teacher, not our undertaker.*
> *Failure is delay, not defeat. It is a temporary detour, not*
> *a dead end. Failure is something we can avoid only by*
> *saying nothing, doing nothing, and being nothing.*
> **Denis Waitley**

Doing something that might contribute to a better and more fulfilling life and failing is better than doing nothing and always wondering and saying, *"I wonder what the outcome would have been if I had tried"*. And, as I said already, failing is not the same as final. You can always start afresh while you are alive. You get one shot at life and every day that you wake up is an opportunity that you are presented to create the life you want – so why not create the life you want? We create the limitation in our minds. We can just as well decide not to limit ourselves. What if you try it and you succeed? What if you start the business and it is a success? What if you go for the audition and you get the acting role? What if you enrol yourself and you get the degree that qualifies you, based on your experience, to get the director job? What if you lose the weight the doctor suggested would greatly contribute to better health? WHAT IF YOU SUCCEED?

> *In any moment of decision, the best thing you can do is the right thing, the next best thing is the wrong thing, and the worst thing you can do is nothing.*
> **Theodore Roosevelt**

So, the stumbling block that you have encountered should not derail you from what you want to achieve. If it means that you have to go back to the drawing board, you go back and make the necessary changes to the plan. Instead of blaming your family for not sending you to university, enrol now and go study part time and, even if it means you complete a 4-year degree in 6 or 7 years, it is way better than the blame game or not taking any action. The benefits of obtaining it eventually, and the advantage and fulfilment it should bring if it were a stumbling block to your goal of getting the promotion, will be way more beneficial than you complaining and blaming your family for another 20 years. This is taking responsibility instead of blaming. This is playing the tokens life dealt you.

Think about it. What does blaming contribute to bettering the situation? There are many people who have done things differently. In fact, I studied for a second qualification and had to attend evening classes while carrying on with my professional and family life during the day. And guess what? I decided to enjoy the 4-year ride. Yes, it took effort. I had to manage my time, I had to contribute financially to pay for my studies, but guess what? I completed it successfully because I was committed to it while also learning something new.

I always believe that I can succeed so, when I take on something, I take it on with that attitude. Before I went to study my degree, I attended a missionary school where I did some short courses on the Bible and some missionary work. I enrolled for my first qualification at a university and completed it in my middle twenties. By then, most of my friends had already completed their studies and were already working. I have "climbed the ladder" and filled employment positions from junior employee to CEO before my middle thirties. I decided to expand my knowledge and professional qualifications in my early thirties and committed to another university qualification. I was approached to sit on a board in my middle thirties. I eventually decided to resign from my employment to pursue my own business. I can go on and on but, through all these stages of my life, I had many people trying to convince me that I should be careful and they tried to make me see my current situation or achievements and why I should not pursue some of these things I have mentioned.

The same applies to taking responsibility for your health. If you do not have time to exercise, make time. Get up an hour earlier every second or third day or go later to bed instead of doing nothing about it or complaining about it. Instead of watching television and claiming it is relaxing after a long day, trade it for exercise that has a benefit to you. Instead of making it a chore, make it part of your lifestyle.

Someone I normally train with and who also introduced me to long distance running once told me that our body is the vehicle that we use to produce out there in the work place, market place, or in whatever we are doing for a living. In other words, his body and mind is what he uses daily to produce. So, he realised from an early age that he has to take care of his body and incorporated exercise and healthy living as a normal part of his lifestyle. I have lost 23 kilograms of weight within 4 months because I was fully committed to the course. Today, learning new skills and living a healthy lifestyle forms part of my life.

> *If you don't like something, change it. If you can't change it, change your attitude.*
> **Maya Angelou**

It's the same with hating your job. Did you ever think of changing jobs or starting a business instead of being unhappy for another 3 years at the same job? Now we can use many other examples, but hopefully you get it: it is taking full responsibility and choosing how you will respond to circumstances and events that are presented to you.

The gentleman I referred to who introduced me to running shared with me that he attends at least three seminars annually and he works it into his budget. He has met many business people at the events he attends and has learned from them, while discovering smarter ways of doing things. Well, one and a half years later, he shared with me that he started to invest in property and he'd bought his first property for rental. In less than a year he bought a second property. I am sharing this with you because he also shared with me that he's decided that he can go with the flow and just work for the rest of his life because he actually enjoys his job, or direct the flow by taking conscious decisions regarding his life and accept responsibility for the decisions and outcomes of his life. Guess what? The small investments he started to make in himself soon started to pay off for him and, even though he is still working, his assets have already start paying him extra cash.

He also shared that another business opportunity was presented to him recently. His view on life has changed and opportunities are presenting themselves and he has developed the eye to see them, asses them and seize each opportunity. But first he took full responsibility for where he was, where he wanted to be and what he needed to do to get where he wanted to be.

How badly do you want to succeed? Remember, take full responsibility for your success, your daily routine, what you allow into your mind, the images you hold in your head, outside influences and your actions and inactions. Remember that you are in control of your choices. You choose whether you will succeed or fail. It is either you who builds the man in the mirror or it is outside influences. You can choose to honestly assess where you are, where you want to be and take full responsibility to get to where you want to be. It is not how you feel; it is a choice that you make to take action towards realizing your dreams. It is not what others think or believe about you; it is what you think and believe about you. And, if that image or thought is negative based on the past, you can still change that thought or image and build a successful future.

Now, let us get back to the questions we asked at the beginning. What does it mean to take full responsibility for your life and how do you take full responsibility for your life?

Taking full responsibility for your life includes being responsible for your thinking and the development of your mind, your feelings, your actions and your words. You take responsibility by managing your thoughts and your mental development through what you allow yourself to read, listen to and meditate on. Taking responsibility is developing a plan for your life. Taking responsibility is accepting the outcomes you are getting and choosing your response and actions to the outcomes. We addressed the mind and thoughts in the previous chapter, but let me say this: what we allow in our mind influences our thinking, feelings, actions and words.

So, from now on, instead of complaining about what life is handing to you, choose to take full responsibility for your response and let your response be the response of a responsible person. The truth is that you have control over the things you are complaining about. Just hear yourself out, whatever the complaint or excuse is. Instead of complaining about how you hate the job, get another job or do something that might make you like your job more; instead of complaining that your clothes are getting too small for you, control your eating habits and exercise or buy new clothes; instead of complaining about people who are taking up your time, tell them that you have important priorities that warrant your time; instead of complaining that you do not have enough money, you either work smarter with the money you have or you go and increase your income. Alternatively you can keep complaining, not get the results you want and regret the life you are living. You make the choice, but my advice to you is to make a choice to create the life you would want to live and commit to creating that life, and to not stop until you reach your goal. I mean, if you are going to live, why not live a good life?

Let me reiterate that I am not saying or suggesting it is going to be an easy or quick road ahead, but embrace the process and learn as you go along and, in doing so, you are writing your own success story.

> *If you own this story, you get to write the ending.*
> **Brene Brown**

Responsibility Poem
Author Unknown

I am responsible

for all that I do,

from turning in work

to making friends, too.

To be kind or mean,

It is up to me

just how much I will learn;

the grades that I get

will be grades that I earn.

I make the choice

to be happy or sad,

to have a good day,

or have one that is bad.

So I will choose

what is best for me.

I am responsible;

I hold the key!

DO YOU KNOW WHERE YOU ARE HEADING?

> *If one advances confidently in the direction of one's dreams, and endeavours to live the life which one has imagined, one will meet with a success unexpected in common hours.*
> **Henry David Thoreau**

I came across an interesting quote from a gentlemen called Lewis Carroll who stated that, "*If you don't know where you are going, any road will get you there*". I want to further add by asking, if you don't know where you are going, how will you know you have arrived at your destination – one you did not plan for or a goal you did not set? This might sound silly to you, but think about it. If I meet you along the road walking somewhere, you will probably be able to tell me where you are going if I ask you. Imagine that I bump into you and ask you where you are going and you tell me, "*Good question, I actually don't know. Can you believe it, I don't actually know where I am going!*" I don't think this would be the case.

Years ago, I was invited to attend a meeting with another two gentlemen who planned to start a business and wanted me to be a third partner in the business. I agreed to meet with them to hear what they had to say. As we opened the meeting, one of the gentlemen ask me a direct question, *"Where are you heading in life?"* He said, "Let me make it more specific: *where do you see yourself in 5 years from now, and do you have a plan to get there?"* He waited for an answer. I knew his reason for asking the question and, even though I could answer him, this question still had me thinking weeks after the meeting.

Now, let me first say that I could see that my response shocked the gentleman because of his facial expression. However, he acted normally. He had not expected the answer I gave him. I set goals, plan on how I will get to my goals and then pursue my goals. I mean, if you are going to do something with your life, why not action your dreams? The reason that made me think about his question was that I got the feeling that he thought he was going to catch me off guard, since the majority of people living today do not have plans or would find it difficult to answer this question, when presented with it.

This brings me back to my question in paragraph one of this chapter. Driven by our daily needs, wants and responsibilities, we might know where we are going when posed the question, *"Where are you going?"* but do we know where we are heading in life? Driven by our daily needs, wants or responsibilities, we know that we are on our way somewhere and if we arrive at that point we see that as achieving the goal. This is whether we are leaving our house to go to the shop, work, gym, visiting friends, holiday, and we can add to the list. However, are we following a plan, blueprint, guideline for our life in order to be clear where we want to be within 5 years from now? Or are we just drifting along, hoping we will arrive at a destination we did not necessary plan for?

I have had the opportunity to work with people who are achievers and go-getters as well as people who are complainers and always see the negative in everything or have an excuse for everything. I decided to engage with the complainers to get to understand them and, as we conversed over time, I started to realise for myself more and more that people do not always know what they want. I further realised that many people are so busy that they don't make time to think or figure out what they want. They are so consumed with life and its challenges that they just push forward, trying to live every day, being busy, but not being purposeful and effective. They are consumed with work, family, debt, social life and other demands.

From my own life experience, I can tell that problems wear a person out and make you tired, especially if you live a purposeless life with no clear direction. Therefore, it is so important to know or be clear regarding the target that you are aiming at: what you want and where you want to be in 5, 10 or 20 years from now. And, when you then know what you are aiming at, you can plan in accordance, start executing and keep focus while slowly drawing closer to the end result. As you go, you can also deal with distractions, roadblocks and difficult circumstances and events, make changes where necessary, and eventually complete or reach your goal.

Whether you like it or not, whether you agree with me or not, the reality is that 5 years from now you will arrive at a certain place in your life. The good news is that you can influence where you will end up then. You can ensure that it is a place you want to be. Alternatively, you can choose to do nothing or just go with the flow and find yourself 5 years down the road at either the place you were 5 years before, with no progress made, a place where small progress has been made that is not necessary satisfying to you but you use this progress to comfort you, or you have advanced by reaching the goals that you have set for yourself. Don't waste another day and year by delaying your dreams. Make up your mind to take action against all odds. Make up your mind to succeed anyway. If you are going to live and take the journey through life, you can just as well make it your goal to enjoy the ride and create the life you want for you and your family.

> *There are many ways of going forward,*
> *but only one way of standing still.*
> **Franklin D. Roosevelt**

Let me give you my personal opinion: I believe every one of us has dreams. We dream of what we really would like to do with our lives. The thing about dreaming is that you think about it and nobody else knows about it unless you share it with them. The reason we have not acted upon it is simply that we believe we will not be able to achieve it, for whatever reason. Perhaps we are too busy, or we think or believe that we are not able to do it, or fear doing it or fear failure. We may fear what others might think and say. Or perhaps we use the age excuse, resources excuse, time excuse, lack of confidence excuse… and so we can add to the list. Some might even worry whether they will be able to make a living from following their passion and dreams.

Forget about any limitations or excuses. It is just you now. So, let me ask you this question: What would you like to do with your life? What is it that you want to achieve in the next 5 years, which will possibly assist you in the future and which you want to build on after the 5 years? What passion drives you and will make you want to get up in the mornings to action the goals you set and the milestones you set for yourself? What is your inner drive that will give you fulfilment and a purpose? Where do you want to end up 5 years from now?

This is where you need to be honest and be true to yourself. Get a quiet place where you can think and reflect; a spot or place where you are alone and where you can forget about the cares of the world, even if it means you have to go to a place that you call your happy place: the beach, mountains, your room, a certain spot in your house, a restaurant, or whatever works for you based on your current circumstances. The point is, make a start.

With many of you, this process will have to be rehearsed a couple of times simply because you need to shift your thoughts from your current realities, to silence the cares, challenges and problems so you can look inside of you and focus on what you really want. This might not be easy, especially if you have been shaped to think a certain way based on different influences such as your environment and upbringing as well as religion. These aforementioned things – coupled with where you find yourself currently in your life, with different responsibilities, problems, challenges, cares, your career or job – might consistently distract you and shout back at you, trying to influence you or overwhelm you, hindering you from seeing yourself as successful.

You might even think that you are silly, trying to participate in such an exercise. You might think that it is not for you, that this is for certain people out there and you are not one of them. Well, you are wrong. Everybody, regardless of where they currently are, can be successful if they follow the principles that govern success and they are willing to work hard and smart. If you are looking at you now, your daily routine will anyway determine where you will be within the next months, year and eventually 5 years. What you do today will influence your future anyway. The difference is that you can now take control of your daily routine by steering it in the direction of your dreams.

In order to steer it in the direction of your dreams, you need to determine what those dreams are. My suggestion to you is that, when you reflect, try to write on a piece of paper what comes to your mind in the first 30 seconds of participating in this exercise, placing no limitations on yourself, with the assumption that you will have all the resources you will need to succeed.

> *Shoot for the moon. Even if you miss,*
> *you'll land among the stars.*
> **Norman Vincent Peale**

How serious are you about succeeding? This is an important question. Is success and the plans you identified for you to pursue a plan B for you, something you hope you will achieve? Or is this your plan A, something you are going to achieve?

When you aim for the target or your identified expected outcome, you cannot go into it half-heartedly. You need a full commitment in order for you to succeed. That is why we start off with identifying what we want, what our target is, what our expected outcome is, what our destination we want to arrive at is. By doing this, we will be clear when we aim and all the things that follow will align to the end results. We will be able to measure progress made in relation to our expected outcome or end result. We will be able to track where we are in relation to our end result, and where we need to make adjustments or alignments we can do so timeously. This also provides us with a degree of certainty. We are clear, we are following a map and we can go back to this map to see if we are on track. We are not shooting in the dark and hoping we will end up somewhere. We are shooting at a target. We are clear as to where we are heading.

So, once again, it might not be easy to at first just come up with this blue-print of what you want, because you are dealing with many influences as indicated earlier. But remember, you are responsible for you, so do not cheat yourself out of the life you want for yourself and your dependants.

All of our situations differ, so you should not waste your time by comparing yourself with others. The only person you should compare yourself with should be you. Yes, you will compare yourself with where you were yesterday, a week ago, a month ago and a year ago. You will track your growth and movement towards your goals. So, be clear as to what you want to achieve, where you want to end up, where you see yourself within the next five years. Remember, you have to document this, write it on a piece of paper, type it on your computer, or capture it on a device that works for you and that you will have access to. You need to document this because this will form part of your plan, which I call your project plan.

Let me repeat again: try to be as clear as possible about where you want to end up. You need to sit still, make time to think, to dream, so that you can know what you want to achieve. Also understand that how we perceive and interpret things has an influence on how we view things that influence our actions. People have their own interpretation or views of what they see, based on their frame of reference, which was framed by different influences. Some of these influences are their upbringing and environment of upbringing, education and development, experiences, religion, and we can add to the list.

You also need to always be true to and honest with yourself. You create the life you want, so don't cheat yourself out of it. See yourself as a person who is important for you. Forget about others; you need to be there for yourself. It might sound selfish, but who will look after you if you are not going to look after you?

When you think about what you want to achieve at this point, forget about the planning, time you will need to work on your desired outcome, resources or anything else you see as an ingredient you will need to achieve your desired outcome. Be true to yourself and think about what you want to achieve. You might come up with 2 or 3 or even 5 things you want to achieve over the next 5 years but, whatever you come up with, write it down so you do not lose track of it. All the other ingredients will follow as soon as you are clear about the target, about what you want to achieve.

Before we look at some examples, I want to share the following. The list below might look like a very pie-in-the-sky type of list which does not necessary comply with the *SMART* principle of setting goals or writing objective statements. I will address the SMART principle in the next chapter, when we deal with setting our goals. In fact, I have come to learn that, when embarking on this process, you should write a first draft, even though it might be a bad draft. Having something on paper is better than having nothing. Having something will allow you to improve upon it and rewrite it to be more measurable. Just by starting, you are already taking a step in the right direction.

With the aforementioned said, take some time to write down some of the dreams that come to mind. It doesn't matter what it is or how simple it might be to you, go for it. Let us look at some examples.

As a first draft, one person might for example choose:

1. Go back to school to finish a degree within the next 5 years;
2. Job promotion;
3. Buy a house in a certain suburb;
4. Improve marriage and relationship with children.

Another person might choose to:

1. Start and grow my own business;
2. Lose weight and become fit as part of a lifestyle;
3. Write a book;
4. Travel overseas.

I don't know what you want and dream about, but you do.

In the next chapter, we will look at making our goals more specific. The planning, action, motivation, management of your time and learning or skills required to make your goal a reality will flow from the clear goal that you set. See yourself as an important person and invest in yourself. Remember, you are going to create the life you want, so set the target for where you want to end up and define your success clearly. Make the investment in yourself by taking the time to reflect, and take the journey of success that you deserve.

> *You don't have to be good to start... you*
> *just have to start to be good!*
> **Joe Sabah**

Don't just Exist
Erin Hanson

So many people walk this earth,
with purpose in their eyes,
But in their heart of hearts they know,
What they're living is a lie.
The alarm goes off at 6am,
Like every other day,
So they can walk into a job they hate,
Because they need the pay.
All time does is take from them,
But it never seems to give.
Always waiting for the day to come,
When they finally start to live.
I'm all too scared that one day soon,
I'll become just like the rest.
Only walking with the crowd,
Because my dreams have been oppressed.
That one day I'll look back on life,
At the opportunities that I missed,
And realize I never truly lived.
All I did was just exist.

Have Specific Goals

> *I don't care how much power, brilliance or energy you have, if you don't harness it and focus it on a specific target, and hold it there, you're never going to accomplish as much as your ability warrants.*
> **Zig Ziglar**

Now that we have addressed the importance of being clear regarding what we want to achieve, let's do it this time by looking at setting some goals. I might repeat some things I addressed in general in the previous chapter, but I want to be more specific and make some examples in this chapter and build on what we have done in the previous chapter. In the previous chapter I set the scene; in this chapter, let us create and document our goals on paper first.

Before we can set the goal, you need to determine what you want. Let me be even clearer by asking you the following question: what exactly is it that you want to achieve? What is the end result you want to accomplish? I will achieve my goal when I:

- Graduate with my degree in law within the next 6 years of part-time studies
- Lose 20 kilograms of weight within the next 6 months

- Read and finish 6 books within the next 6 months as part of my self-development
- Start my own clothing brand and sell it online within the next 12 months

I recently, while writing this section of the book, also wrote an exam on a business course I am busy studying. One of the questions was to develop SMART objectives for a business. They provided us with a scenario and I had to indicate if it complied with the SMART principle or not. I enjoyed the task because I believe that applying the SMART principle as part of the ingredients for success is important. So, what does SMART stand for?

S – *Specific*
M – *Measurable*
A – *Attainable*
R – *Relevant*
T – *Time-Bound*

Specific – Clearly stipulate what needs to be accomplished. Instead of just generalizing, be specific. An example is when you say I want to lose weight versus I want to lose 20 kilograms within the next six months.

Measurable – Benchmark that will allow you to evaluate to determine when you completed the goal. It will also allow you to measure progress made towards your goal. It allows you to set and measure progress on milestones. You can measure daily, weekly, monthly, 2-monthly, up to the 6 month mark. It allows you to also make necessary changes where necessary, early in the process.

Attainable – The likelihood that you will achieve the goal, taking into consideration your relevant knowledge and resources. Set a goal that will be challenging, but make sure that you can see yourself achieving the set goal. Can you see yourself losing 20 kilograms and will you commit to doing so?

Relevant – The goal is important and contributes to your life objectives. By pursuing this goal, it will contribute to my health positively. It will increase my energy levels which will assist with productivity in my career, business and family life.

Time-Bound – Time allocated to complete the goal. We allocated 6 months to achieve the goal.

So the goal that we set to lose 20 kilograms of weight within the next 6 months is a simple goal that complies with the SMART principle. Being clear about what you want already helps you with the plan to get what you want.

So let us try this again by asking specific questions to help us set our goal clearly.

S – SPECIFIC	What do you want to accomplish? Can I quantify? By when?
	• *I want to lose weight.* • *20 kilograms.* • *6 months from 10 January 2019 which is 10 July 2019.*
M – MEASURABLE	How will I measure my progress or know that I have reached my goal …?
	By determining what my weight is on 10 January 2019 and documenting it. I will measure progress regularly by weighing myself on a scale as required by my milestones, e.g. weekly, and finally at the end of the 6 months – at 07:00 on 10 July 2019 – to determine my progress against my set goal. I can capture my progress weekly to measure movement towards my goal.
A – ATTAINABLE	Do you have the skills or can you obtain the skills necessary for you to reach the goal within the set time-frames. Do you have the resources? Will you cope with any amount of effort required to reach the goal?
	Losing 20 kilograms of weight within 6 months. If I follow a healthy diet and exercise regularly, I will be able to reach the set goal. To exercise I have different options: • Get a personal trainer • Join a gym and exercise on my own

A – ATTAINABLE **(continued)**	• Run or cycling regularly outside rather than joining a gym • Take daily walks of 30 minutes instead of running • Follow a cardio exercise programme on YouTube I will work out a diet plan for me by: • Seeing my physician or a dietician • Buying a book on healthy living and exercise • Reading articles on the internet • Watching YouTube videos to educate me • Speaking to friends or colleagues who are more knowledgeable and are currently participating in healthy living. You will have to choose from the list above. For example, you make the choice to run outside. In the next chapter we will interrogate this in more detail as it deals with planning. You will also have to make time in your daily program to accommodate the choice you make for exercise, budget for your choice of diet, and make time to prepare your dietary requirements.
R – RELEVANT	Why did I set this goal and how does it align to my life objectives? Pursuing this goal will contribute to my health positively. It will increase my energy levels, which will assist with productivity in my career, business and family life.

	What is the end date or deadline for the goal? Is the time realistic?
T – TIME-BOUND	6 months to achieve the goal (*6 months from 10 January 2019 which is 10 July 2019*). Referring to attainable column, it is realistic and can be attained.
GOAL – SMART	Lose 20 kilograms of weight within the next 6 months

If you are clear about what you want, your planning will also be more effective because you know what you are aiming for. It will further influence and provide clarity for what you should action daily, weekly and monthly. It allows you to schedule your day in order to ensure you have control over your actions and by doing this you create order and the possible guarantee that you will reach your goal. In other words, if you have a 5-year goal, you break it up into smaller achievable time-lines within the 5 years. Within the time-lines, you set activities with deadlines. Remember, what you do daily contributes to your goal. So your daily routine is important and you reach your goal by taking daily action that will contribute to weekly, monthly and annual progress towards the end result. Which brings me to my next point: writing down your goal.

I have heard people say, "My goal is in my head. I know what I want." The problem with not documenting it is that you can forget it or lose track of it. I suggest that you write your goals down or capture them on an electronic device such as a computer or phone. Writing your goals down provides you with the opportunity to make them as clear as possible and provides you with a blueprint of what you want to achieve. You can go and refer back to it regularly to keep you on track. It will assist you in developing achievable milestones and to organize your activities around these goals. This will contribute to order in your life. It will assist with developing a roadmap for your destination that you have identified. It will assist with planning the actions you will take to bring the plan to fruition. It will act as a reminder of why you are doing what you are doing, and it will act as a motivation.

Many people hesitate to set goals or do not set goals because they can immediately see the obstacles that in their opinion might hinder them from achieving the goal they want to pursue. These obstacles might be real, but that doesn't mean that it should stop you from achieving your goals. You still set the goal, and then you identify the obstacles. The obstacles should therefore not stop you from setting the goal because, if you identify the obstacle, you can look at solutions to address or deal with the obstacles you have identified. Obstacles are something that can be addressed if you are determined to achieve the goal.

> *Success is no accident. It is hard work, perseverance, learning, studying, sacrifice and, most of all, love of what you are doing or learning to do.*
> **Pele**

So, you want to complete a law degree within the next 6 years of part-time studies. Your financial situation is such that you cannot afford to pay for the university fees and your setup at home is that you cannot study because of your children or other interferences. Engage with the university regarding different payment plans; engage with bursars for bursaries; hear whether your employer is willing to pay for you; hear from family members if they are willing to assist you; restructure your finances so that when you get your annual increase you can use it for the payment at the university; approach businesses to hear if they are willing to sponsor you; do extramural activities to support your university fees; and so we can have more creative ways of trying to address the identified obstacle. With regards to the interferences or hindrances in your home setup, identify whether you have a library in your area; get up earlier or go to bed later; stay an hour later after work every day to put in some work; use a family member's house, the local church or the university campus.

I have experienced that, when I set a goal, I make a decision that I am going to achieve that goal. After I've made the decision to take full responsibility to reach the goal and I have defined the goal clearly, only then do I identify the obstacles. Now, I do not see these obstacles as constraints or limitations because I will search for ways to address the obstacles and see this as part of the journey. I also see this as an opportunity to grow, to think, to solve a problem, and this part of the journey will contribute to my story when I achieve the goal. So, do not create limitations before you even set your goal, and do not let your limiting beliefs interfere with your deciding on and setting your goals.

Identify who your important stakeholders are. You need to consult or include them on the journey to achieving your goal. This can be family members, your banker, lecturers, spouse, your boss, clients, business partners, and so on. Also identify what their roles are on your journey to your success. If we use the last example, if you are going to study part time you need to inform your boss that you will need time off to go and write exams and tests or that you will be applying for time off to study. This is an opportunity to sell your goal to him or her. Your husband or wife plays an important role in supporting you and taking care of the children. If you are going to take a loan for the studies, you need to liaise with your banker. As time progresses, you build relationships with the lecturers and other students with whom you might form study groups and participate with in group assignments.

I heard a preacher once say that no one can make it on his or her own. We all need people. And he further made examples by saying that, when your car breaks down and you do not know how to fix it, you need someone to come and help you. It takes two people to bring a third life into this world. So, building positive relationships with relevant stakeholders in pursuing your goals will be of great assistance to you.

Now, you might get some instances where someone will not want to be of assistance to you, but we dealt with obstacles and, as I said before, I don't see obstacles as constraints or limitations because I will search for ways to address the obstacles and see this as part of the journey. You have set the target, so you either jump over the hurdle, go around it or go under it, and then you continue running.

When you have identified your goals and you have documented the goals, you need to break them into achievable milestones.

In the next section, under planning, I will explain how to break each goal up into a detailed plan with milestones and time-lines as an example and for illustration purposes. We will also practically include the last four paragraphs above by illustrating how we identify obstacles and identify our stakeholders or those who are important people in our journey towards our goal.

> *The trouble with not having a goal is that you can spend your life running up and down the field and never score.*
> **Bill Copeland**

My Wages
Jessie B. Rittenhouse

I bargained with Life for a penny,
And Life would pay no more,
However I begged at evening
When I counted my scanty store;

For Life is just an employer,
He gives you what you ask,
But once you have set the wages,
Why, you must bear the task.

I worked for a menial's hire,
Only to learn, dismayed,
That any wage I had asked of Life,
Life would have paid.

PLANNING

> *A goal without a plan is just a wish.*
> **Antoine de Saint-Exupéry**

You might have heard the saying by Benjamin Franklin, "If you fail to plan, you are planning to fail". In the previous chapter we worked through setting a goal using the SMART principle. You can set a goal, *"Lose 20 kilograms of weight within the next 6 months"*, but that goal will not be achieved automatically. You need a plan to guide your action in order for you to reach the goal. You are clear about your end result, but you need to have corresponding action that will bring you to the end result.

That is why people set New Year's resolutions and do not follow through on them. They did not plan how they would go about achieving the goal or resolution and, in the absence of a clear plan, they soon fell back into their old schedule because they did not have a blueprint that they had committed to follow – a blueprint that guides them every day. The next year they do it again and they repeat the cycle. You need to be conscious about your life.

Bill Gates said, *"Most people overestimate what they can do in one year and underestimate what they can do in ten years"*. What you do daily matters. That's why you have to plan your day, otherwise it will be wasted on irrelevant tasks or others will plan it for you. Plan your day and stick to the plan. The good thing about planning your day is that you can plan it the way you want it. You know your peak energy times and lower energy times. Even if you do not stick to the whole schedule, at least you will have made a start, and a little progress in the right direction is better than no progress at all. Tomorrow you come back and better your record of the day before. You might hit a strike rate of 60% today. Well, 60% is better than an unproductive day. A 60% strike rate in the direction of your goal is better than a 0% strike rate where you are directionless. I like the saying or quote by Lao Tzu that goes, "A journey of a thousand miles begins with one step".

I had a lecturer who taught me statistics. He once told us that compound interest is a wonderful thing for the person who benefits from it. When he encouraged the class, he used to say that 1% positive increase towards your plans is better than 0%, and 2% increase is better than 1%. He said that it may seem small and insignificant, but if you consistently put it in, it will eventually compound and the 4% becomes 8%. So, even if you make small steps upwards, as long as there is growth, as long as you better your record of yesterday and do not slip back, you are growing. And, even if you fall back, tomorrow is a new day to make a fresh start and make progress again.

It is very important, though, that we make sure we are on the right track, and not a track leading us away from our goals. What do I mean? That is why I said we need to sit still and think. We need to define our end result and, based on our end result, we need to plan our route to get to our end result. We do not want to travel half way and then realise we are moving away from our destination, from our set goal, our determined outcome, rather than towards it.

Planning allows you to establish and lay out the route for travelling towards your goal or your desired outcome. In other words, it allows you to think through how you are going to reach the goal that you set or the desired outcome you have identified. It allows you to document the plan and break it down into your daily tasks in order for you to work towards your goal or desired outcome. It is a blueprint that you can use to get back on track. It is your motivation as to what you are heading towards when doubt and lack of purpose makes its appearance. Planning will draw ideas out of you that will build even further on your goals. It also provides structure as to how you will use your resources, such as time and money, and allows you to set deadlines for your goals and the daily or weekly milestones you set for yourself that contribute to your goals or planned outcomes.

Planning makes you to think though concepts and processes clearly and draw a sketch from start to finish while identifying risk factors, but it also allows you to eventually narrow your options and choose the option best suited to you. This should influence your decisions and actions to contribute to a bigger purpose – the long-term perspective – which provides your purpose and fulfilment in the present and a clear sense as to what you are working towards. It allows you to make intelligent decisions now to steer you towards that goal that you set out to reach within 3, 4 or 5 years from now. It allows us to take stock and identify and eliminate actions not contributing towards our goals.

Planning grants us the opportunity to break our goals up into smaller, achievable milestones. Planning allows you to schedule your day to allocate time to work on your milestones. Planning creates order and grants you the opportunity to schedule your day in such a way that you have a high probability of reaching your goal. It identifies in which areas you need to develop yourself in order to reach your goal.

> *Plan your work and work your plan.*
> **Napoleon Hill**

Let us use the same example from the previous chapter and build on it.

S – SPECIFIC	What do you want to accomplish? Can I quantify? By when?
	I want to lose weight. 20 kilograms. 6 months from 10 January 2019 which is 10 July 2019.
M – MEASURABLE	How will I measure my progress or know I have reached my goal?
	By determining what my weight is on 10 January 2019 and documenting it. I will measure progress regularly by weighing myself as required by my milestones, e.g. weekly, and finally, at the end of the 6 months, at 07:00 on 10 July 2019 to determine my progress against my set goal. I can capture my progress weekly to measure movement towards my goal.
A – ATTAINABLE	Do you have or can you obtain the skills necessary for you to reach the goal within the set time-frames. Do you have the resources? Will you cope with any amount of effort required to reach the goal?
	Losing 20 kilograms within 6 months. If I follow a healthy diet and exercise regularly, I will be able to reach the set goal. To exercise I have different options:

A – ATTAINABLE (continued)	• Get a personal trainer • Join a gym and exercise on my own • Run regularly outside rather than joining a gym • Take daily walks of 30 minutes instead of running I will work out a diet plan for me by: • Seeing my physician or a dietician • Buying a book on healthy living and exercise • Reading articles on the internet • Watching YouTube videos to educate me • Speaking to friends or colleagues who are more knowledgeable and are currently participating in healthy living.
R – RELEVANT	Why did I set this goal and how does it align to my life objectives?
	By pursuing this goal, it will contribute to my health positively. It will increase my energy levels, which will assist with productivity in my career, business and family life.
T – TIME-BOUND	What is the end date or deadline for the goal? Is the time realistic?
	6 months to achieve the goal. Referring to attainable column, it is realistic and can be attained.
GOAL – SMART	Lose 20 kilograms of weight within the next 6 months

Let us use the same example from the previous chapter and build on it while we set a plan in place. This is to illustrate the process and it does not matter what your goals are. The research might differ but the principle remains the same.

My goal is to lose 20 kilograms of weight within the next 6 months. In my planning, I need to determine what needs to happen in order for me to reach my goal. What are the actions that I must take in order to bring my goals to fruition? If we are clear and have determined our actions, we will capture it into a schedule and make sure we follow through on our schedule.

So, what are milestones then? We have set the goal as our end result. A milestone is simply a smaller, more manageable deadline, with time-lines for us to achieve it. A milestone manages movement and tracks progress towards our goal. It allows us to break the end result into smaller, manageable activities and allows us to celebrate smaller victories on our way to the bigger goal. It allows us to see progress made towards our goal as well as to identify and assess complications and make the necessary changes to address such complications. This might be simply adjusting the plan or changing our strategy altogether.

So, if you want to reach your goal, you need to determine what the important factors that will play a role in you achieving your goal are. What you will eat is important. Physical exercise will assist you with reaching your goal. You need time to exercise. You need exercise clothes like running gear, shoes, pants, t-shirt, socks, or a bicycle and cycling gear, depending on what exercise you will pursue.

Let's say you have decided to run outside. If you want data relating to your running, such as the time you're running or calories lost, you can either use a sports watch or your phone by downloading an app. You might need extra money for a new diet, or you could just change your current buying list to accommodate healthier foods.

The good thing about planning is that you can weigh up your options and check them against reality. For example, you can simply go and see a dietician to work out a eating plan for you. You could speak to your trainer, if you choose to hire a professional trainer, and get advice from the trainer regarding a diet for you. Or you could Google an eating plan.

The same goes for your training. You can either choose to appoint a professional trainer, train with a group of friends as an encouragement for you to train, or decide to train by yourself. You can decide to join a gym to make use of their equipment. You can buy a bicycle and cycle while adding some weight training, or you can choose to run and even do some fun runs as you get better. Depending on your time and financial situation, you will decide what will work for you. The point is, you have a number of ways you can approach your goal. Where you find yourself at the moment will determine which one you will choose.

After carefully considering your options, let's say you have decided to exercise on your own. You have decided that for the next 6 months you will run outdoors and after the 6 months you will assess your progress against your set goal. You have decided that for the first month you will run or walk 8 kilometres. You will do 2 days on and one day off. You will also plan your eating schedule for yourself and stick to it. You will run every morning between 05:30 and 06:30. You have documented your running schedule something like this:

January 2019					
Date	Day	Kms run	Time	Min/Kim	Weight (kg)
10	Thursday				
11	Friday				
13	Sunday				
14	Monday				
16	Wednesday				
17	Thursday				
19	Saturday				
20	Sunday				
22	Tuesday				
23	Wednesday				
25	Friday				
26	Saturday				
28	Monday				
29	Tuesday				
31	Thursday				

Above is the schedule for the first period and after every run you will complete the schedule. It will allow you to track certain information. You need to commit to the schedule and complete the data every day. This will be your routine for the next 6 months, as set out in your goal.

It might seem like a fruitless exercise. Why not just hit the road and run and see what happens? By getting into this habit of documenting this exercise, you will actually have data that tells a story from which you can analyse and measure input versus output. When engaging with others, you will have a story to tell to them based on the data you have captured.

> *The world makes way for the man who knows where he is going.*
> **Ralph Waldo Emerson**

This exercise that we have completed is an easy exercise. You can use this same approach to assist you in documenting other goals. It doesn't matter what these goals are. Whether it is pursuing a promotion, starting your business, making a million within the next 12 months or buying your own house within the next 3 years, document it and get to work by sticking to the plan and aligning the plan when you need to.

The value of planning how you will operate each day is that it allows you to schedule the hour you set out for this output into your day. In this case, we scheduled it for 05:30 in the morning. You can go to your schedule to identify when you are on or when you are off. It is now not just in your head, but also on paper and it tells a story that you can share with someone else to motivate, when the need arises.

Let's say that you have committed to the first month of running or walking. Below is an example of your completed planning schedule for January.

January 2019					
Date	Day	Kms run	Time	Min/Kim	Weight (kg)
10	Thursday	8.04	48.38	6.03	100
11	Friday	7.83	46.14	5.54	100
13	Sunday	8.00	49.59	6.14	99.2
14	Monday	7.93	50.03	6.18	99.4
16	Wednesday	8.92	56.46	6.21	98.5
17	Thursday	8.48	51.17	6.02	98.6
19	Saturday	7.96	50.30	6.20	98.1
20	Sunday	8.88	54.04	6.05	97.7
22	Tuesday	7.96	46.23	5.49	97.9
23	Wednesday	8.52	48.33	5.41	97.1
25	Friday	8.73	52.16	5.59	96.7
26	Saturday	8.07	47.12	5.51	96.4
28	Monday	7.93	50.03	6.18	96.1
29	Tuesday	8.01	48.49	6.05	95.6
31	Thursday	7.83	46.14	5.54	95.5

By looking at the above completed schedule, you will now see that you can actually track and analyse some data. You will do exactly the same for the month of February up to June. You will also do the same regarding your eating schedule. It is no use running and not eating the food that will assist you with losing weight. Sticking to the schedule will be important. So put this into practice and see what will happen if you act.

Believe In Yourself
By Sagar

Believe in yourself and you can achieve
Things you never thought possible.
Believe in yourself and you can discover
New talents hidden inside of you.

Believe in yourself and you can reach
New heights that you thought immeasurable.
Believe in yourself and you can elucidate
The problem that defies every solution.

Believe in yourself and you can tackle
The hardest of all situations.
Believe in yourself and you can make
The complicated things seem simple.

Believe in yourself and you can enjoy
The beauty of nature's creation.
Believe in yourself and you can learn
Skills of gaining knowledge from experience.

Believe in yourself and you can discern
New depths in your life.
Believe in yourself and you can perform
Way beyond your expectations.

Believe in your aim and work towards it,
With elation, determination and dedication.
Believe in yourself and you'll feel blessed,
As you are God's special creation.

Taking Corresponding Action

Action is the foundational key to all success.
Pablo Picasso

In order to succeed at anything, you have to act upon the principles that govern the outcome of what you want. You also need to be consistent. As stated in a previous chapter, unfortunately many people get excited for a while and decide they want a certain outcome. They start dreaming about this outcome, and repeat this action every year as a new year resolution. Years have passed, without any action. You get many *"going to do"* people.

I saw a post of a quote from an unknown author which states that *"You can't plough a field simply by turning it over in your mind"*. You plough that field by taking action. You need to take daily action. You need to produce and be equipped for today, yet ensure that you grow to meet the demands and trends of the future. You might be knowledgeable today, but with trends and technology changing rapidly, continuous education and self-development is essential in order to be relevant for the future.

I have heard many people before saying, "But I know that". I think to myself, "If you know it, why don't you do it or apply it?" Knowing it does not make the difference. Taking action will make the difference. So, you might know what you need to do to get the outcome, such as losing 20 kilograms of weight. But knowing what to do does not bring the results. It is important to know, but it is the knowing and the right attitude, coupled with consistent action, that will bring the results.

How we see things motivates our actions. Therefore, we can influence how we see things by replacing old information with new information. Personal effectiveness requires continuous growth and consistency of purpose. Many people want to look successful out there, by acting successful, but acting can only last for so long before the real you will surface. Instead of trying to show people out there what you achieved, you need to succeed privately, and your success will speak for itself. It is small victories of getting up in time and taking the consistent actions required that will eventually show results, and others will start to see it.

It is important to evaluate or determine from time to time our progress made and be self-aware of our daily actions and our habits. And whatever situations or experiences we go through, it is important that we take out the lessons learned for moving forward. Examining yourself regularly and honestly, and evaluating and viewing your actions against your end result or goal, is important to keep you on track, but also to become aware again of where you are heading and what you need to do to get there. Small consistent and planned actions eventually add up to tangible results and lead to reaching the goal.

You need to look after you. You need to take care of yourself, treat yourself and develop yourself. If you are not going to do it, no one else will. Make it a goal to grow and learn daily. Start to apply what you learn, and you will be amazed at yourself in one year from now.

With the technology of today, there are many ways to develop oneself. Choose a medium that works for you, whether it be reading a book for 30 minutes a day, listening to a motivational talk, YouTube talks, blogs, audio books or whatever.

The taking action part is often the delaying factor, since we are afraid of failing. My response to the question, "But what if I fail?" is normally, "But what if you succeed?" If you do not take action, you will not know. You should not go into something with a negative, defeated attitude, because you have then already set the trend for failure.

Assuming that you have applied all the aforementioned processes in the foregoing chapters so far, now it is time to get to work. Success requires action. Ever heard someone ask, *"What is your plan of action?"* The plan that you documented, without corresponding action, equals no movement towards your planned outcomes or goals. And yes, your action should be action that corresponds to the documented plan you have developed. This should actually make it easier because the documented plan will provide you with a sense of direction, and people are more relaxed or at ease when they have a sense of direction or a blueprint to follow. People are afraid of the unknown and want order rather than chaos. The reality, however, is that success will require you to get out of your comfort zone and, in many instances, people stop here because it is the taking action, the doing part that puts them off.

> *Your future is being created through the actions you take today.*
> **Clyde Lee Dennis**

Let me say this: starting off in many instances might be the hardest part for many, because up to now you have got yourself into a space of self-belief, dreaming, planning, refining your goals to be specific, and documenting the plan into achievable milestones with resource requirements and due dates. In essence, you actually have your project plan to clearly guide you through the process from point A to point B, with potential identified risk factors and possible mitigating factors to address these risk factors. You are good to go – yet many people get stuck at this point, the point of taking action or getting started.

It might be that your mind is asking you why you are doing this. Negative thoughts might be flashing through your mind. Self-doubt and fear might start to kick in. It might be a little uncomfortable to get started: to run on the road and after the first 30 seconds feel like your lungs want to jump out of your chest. Going for the first time to the buyers to negotiate a good price for the products you plan to buy and sell. Enrolling to get that qualification. Registering the business.

I am not sure what journey you are embarking on, but one thing I can tell you: if you have documented the plan, follow though. Giving up should never be an option. This is critical. Your outcome a year from now will be determined by you making the move as planned – or not making the move. This decision is a matter of you reaching that goal or not, living that fulfilled life or not. It is in your hands.

Something that helped me greatly on my journey was that years ago I discovered that people are basically just people and I refuse to allow any person to place a worth on me. Everyone started somewhere and you might be at the starting point at this stage. I respect people and their opinions, but I will determine my own realities and will not take action based on people's opinions regarding me. I will ensure that I always develop myself so I can make informed decisions. Now, I will constantly evaluate my actions and where I need to make changes I will.

What do I mean? All of us are human beings. I started off this book by addressing the mind and how you see yourself. Let me remind you of the quote of a gentlemen called W. Clement Stone, who said: *"There is little difference in people,* *but that little difference makes a big difference. The little difference is attitude. The big difference is whether it is **positive or negative**."*

It has been said that it is during take-off that an aircraft uses most of its power and, when lifted into the air and flying, it reduces its power. So it is the take-off, getting up in the air, that requires more power but, when it is up there, it requires less power. My advice to you is, get started and you will soon become stronger and better. You will not only become stronger and better, but you will become more confident. You will grow though the process and sooner or later you will start embarking on new ventures and expanding your goals and dreams.

> *There are only two rules for being successful. One, figure out exactly what you want to do, and two, do it.*
> **Mario Cuomo**

I like how Eddie Rickenbacker puts it: *"I can give you a six-word formula for success: Think things through – then follow through."*

In this section of this book, we are addressing taking action. However, the steps foregoing this step made us think through what we want, and we have documented it in a way using the SMART principal and have broken it down into milestones and daily tasks in order to eat the elephant one bite at a time. Many people, many times, get here and action is now required. It is the action, the follow through, that will make the foregoing processes a tangible reality. A person who is determined to succeed will succeed against all odds and, if we don't see a way in front of us, we either make a way or find a way. The people you see as successful today also had to start somewhere. If you get to know them you will realize that they probably failed at many things and in some instances had more than one attempt at some significant achievements, but they never gave up. They persevered in spite of all the odds that might have been against them.

If you are employed at this stage, just imagine: if the owner of the company had not taken action, the company would have not be there. If I had not written this book, you would not have read it. So, there might be more than just you depending on what you think might be insignificant.

It is the daily action that you take that will contribute to the weekly progress, that will advance to the monthly outcomes, that will translate into the change and progress that you can see, that will require you to rework the goal to expand because of the significant growth... and soon you will return to the drawing board to re-adjust the plans and expand on the goal because of the significant growth... and all of this because you decided to follow through and took action. The once-upon-a-time plan that was documented will now become alive and a reality.

Others might not have seen the goal when you started off, while all this was a reality for you from the start inside of you, and what you saw inside of you has now been translated into the outside world.

When people ask you questions such as, "When did this happen?" you should take them back to the start, when you had your first rough draft of the plan, and explain how you refined it to make it more specific, until you had your blueprint of how you saw it and it became a reality for you before it was even started in the natural world or action was taken towards the goals externally.

What I am saying is, if you can see it, if it becomes real to you, with the corresponding action and perseverance it will become a reality soon for the rest of the world.

> *You are what you do, not what you say you do.*
> **Carl Jung**

So, if you are committed to the course, and you take the corresponding action, the results will follow. You need to make up your mind that quitting is not an option. How you feel does not determine your daily action. You do what you have to do every day, whether you feel like it or not. Jerry West said, *"You can't get much done in life if you only work on the days you feel good"*.

Make that start, take action, and soon you will live your dreams.

They called it luck
Author Unknown

He worked by day
and toiled by night.

He gave up play
and some delight.

Dry books he read,
new things to learn.

And forged ahead,
success to earn.

He plodded on,
With faith and pluck;

And when he won,
they called it luck.